A MARRIAGE OF POETS

Arthur and Kit Knight

with a foreword by
James Drought

SPOON RIVER POETRY PRESS
PEORIA, ILLINOIS
1984

This book is published in part with funds provided by the Illinois Arts Council, a state organization, and by the National Endowment for the Arts. Our many thanks.

A *Marriage of Poets* copyright (C) 1984 by Arthur & Kit Knight, all rights reserved. No portion of this book may be reproduced in any manner without written permission of the authors, except for quotations embodied in reviews or critical articles.

Published by Spoon River Poetry Press, David Pichaske, editor; P. O. Box 1443; Peoria, Illinois 61655. Typesetting by D. J. Graphics, Peoria, Illinois; printing and binding by M. & D. Printers, Henry, Illinois.

ISBN 0-933180-61-6

A MARRIAGE OF POETS

A Look at Arthur and Kit Knight
    by James Drought   v

Honeymoons	1
Is the Garbage on Fire Yet?	3
Philosophy	4
Fat	5
The Buy	6
Breast-feeding	7
A Great Place To Be	8
The Magic Day	10
Scars	11
Russian Christmas	12
John Wayne is Dying	13
A Valentine's Day Poem for Mark	14
Sweet Potato	15
That Clean Sun Smell	19
Woman of the Year	20
Symbols	22
Memorial Day	23
Memorial Day Rose	24
The Picnic	25
Specific Detail	26
Destruction	28
The Result	29
Constellations	30
His Grandson Is Uneasy	31
The Cache	32
Summer Roses	33
The Breakdown	34
A Nice Thing To Do	35
Promise Me	37
Horror Stories	38
Kevin	39
Two Women	40

The Thief	42
Breakfast	43
Petting	44
Bananas Are for Dead People	45
Bailing	46
The Queen Lives on Unemployment	47
Simple Things	48
Up With the Bourgeois	49
On the Road	50
Ink Stains	51
Denial	52
Too Old to Be Sexy	53

A LOOK AT ARTHUR AND KIT KNIGHT
by James Drought

During the past two decades in the U. S., the writing of poetry, which had previously been the preserve of an elite group of academically-supported versifiers, opened itself up to include a great mass of young people who treated poetry as a folk art dealing almost exclusively in a casual conversational expression of common experience. This "popular" poetry, a sort of condensed, spaced-out prose, was made to be spoken rather than sung (or, as in the case of older academic poets, thought), and it became the carrier of the random opinions of the youngest adult generations among us.

Some people suggest that this new poetry arrived as a natural progeny of the Beat writers—Allen Ginsberg, Lawrence Ferlinghetti, Jack Kerouac, Neal Cassady, Gary Snyder, Kenneth Rexroth et al. Other researchers place the new poetry as the simple result of a watering down process of instruction that our writing classes engaged in so that they could contain the increasing numbers of neophyte poets who flooded the colleges and universities after World War II because of educational bonuses for returning veterans. Some people say a casualness in the new poetry simply represented a new unrestricted way of American life riding the prosperity wake of a 30-year postwar economic boom.

Whatever the reason, it is upon us. Vast numbers of creditable poets are practicing without ever having to scan a line of verse, who know nothing of the traditional poetic forms. A Bob Dylan, for instance, or a Patti Smith, fits lyrics to simple melodies backed up by a few repetitive chords. A Lyn Lifshin delights us by manipulating the spacing on her typewriter. Mike Hogan sometimes even drops the pose of poet and proffers his musical memories in condensed prose cadenzas without batting an eye. Of course, there are exceptions to these casual trends—Virginia Rudder can still thrill us with a modern-day woman's message ensconced in the sweeping rhythms of an Aeschylean chorus; but not often do we read or hear anything that breaks the new conversational trend randomly delivered. In Marvin Malone's *Wormwood Review*, one encounters very fine poetry, but all of it sounds as if it were written by the same person. Don't misunderstand me, this is not an unusual phenomenom—In feudal France and England during the time of the great lute-playing troubadours, no attempt was made to depart from a commonly accepted style. I doubt if anyone can spot individual stylistic devices in the great Gregorian chants—who would want to?

Personally, I don't believe the new poetry can be attributed to The Beats. Ginsberg, Ferlinghetti, even Snyder, and certainly Rexroth, were, and are, all very classic in their techniques. The early

Ginsberg of "Howl" harked back to rhythms established by Walt Whitman and formalized by Vachel Lindsay. Ferlinghetti's work whispers its technical derivations from the great Italians, Dante, and even D'Annunzio and Petrarch. Snyder and the recent Ginsberg are using well-established oriental verse forms of Japan, China and India. No, the Beats cannot take the credit for this new popular conversational poetic style, although certainly they interested great numbers of young people during the 1950s in the very existence of poetry and the practice of it, particularly the performing of it personally on a stage rather than in an academically-subsidized review magazine. The new poetry was printed by typewriter and made public through the poet's mouth to all who were willing to listen. This, I believe, is what caused it to become conversational—the fact that it had to be personally performed.

Most of the young poets in the 1950s became poets *because* they could *not* play a musical instrument. They did not think to accompany themselves on anything, and knowing nothing of music, they did not choose to sing. They simply chanted, intoned, or spoke. They believed that what they were saying about themselves was important! A belief that succeeding American generations of the 1960s and 1970s were to embrace with growing self-indulgent fervor, spurred on by an educational system that had adapted to the flooding numbers by encouraging personal expression as a way of communicating. With the establishment of the endowment-subsidies in the late 1960s, this popular stage-chatter began to appear in printed magazines, books, all financed by federal and state tax money. It became what the young thought of as Poetry itself, capitalized in print forever.

Arthur Winfield Knight is one of the best of these new casual poets. In short directly-stated speech, using fewer metaphors than even William Carlos Williams ever allowed himself, Knight stamps home to us a humane concerned life among others who seem to surprise him with their agonies and self-lies. His narrator, however, takes the same attitude toward himself—treating his somewhat ordinary experiences with a slight disdain. If Knight's pity is in somewhat short supply, it is probably because his personal life has been filled with harsh psychologically unbearable events, and they robbed him of the sentimentality shared by most of our poets his age. Becoming an adult some twenty-five years ago, Knight married too quickly and suffered the hopelessness of extreme poverty. He married again, after his first marriage was annulled, and promptly went through the hell of his second wife's derangement. The third wife he took was irrevocably dying from the moment they met, and Knight found himself absorbed in nursing her unselfishly until she succumbed.

When his third wife died, one would think that Arthur would relievedly retire to a hermitage, but instead he embarked on a new relationship with one of his former students, Kit, whose previous life had been no picnic either—she had survived a near fatal car accident and fought her way back to recovery in what must have seemed like an endless number of operations, then made a disastrous marriage to an Air Force sergeant before freeing herself. Both of the Knights now seem unbelievably happy with one another, a happiness that they deliberately craft for themselves efficiently, since they are both experienced in the disasters that mistakes can lead to. These are people who don't make mistakes anymore—they run their press, *unspeakable visions of the individual*, together, and they have already published four volumes of their Beat journals, as well as some very fine pamphlets and chapbooks: one a sensitive memoir of Jack Kerouac by John Clellon Holmes.

But if Arthur's poetry tells us of an odyssey through personal torture toward ultimate happiness, Kit's conversational poems are concerned very little with her past life. Like a combination of Colette—providing the most intimate details of a modern wife's and mother's life—and Dorothy Parker—brilliant wit going off like fireworks on a black July sky—she delights her audience by casting ordinary events with great precision and humor. Kit Knight can be said to write barbs. Together, the Knights make barbed wire—Arthur contributing a strong unbroken continuum, while Kit's comments cause explosive points to occur periodically. We get to see what would have happened if William Carlos Williams had married Dorothy Parker, or Paul Valery had gotten mixed up with Colette. Arthur and Kit Knight are a very exciting pair—something like the young Lunts, only of Literature.

But not enough has been said of their publishing venture, *unspeakable visions of the individual*, named after a phrase from Jack Kerouac's work. As a young photographer in the San Francisco area (he took the well-used photo of Henry Miller in the black and white checkered shirt), Arthur was thought to be a very ingratiating but brilliantly talented young man by the older Beats (if this is what the likes of Henry Miller could be called). He gathered information and pictures of them, as well as their unpublished personal writings, much the way his father gathered specimens of the fauna and flora of California for the East Bay Regional Park System, where he worked. In 1974 Arthur decided to publish some of his Beat Collection in *The Beat Book*. Since then, with Kit, he has published three more volumes—*The Beat Diary, The Beat Journey* and *unspeakable visions*, 10th anniversary issue. These books are an invaluable raw history of the Beats' experiences through their own words and pictures. (One sees personal photographs of his wife, Carolyn, taken in off moments by Neal Cassady, accompanied by a ruthlessly truthful memoir of Cassady, Kerouac and those times by Carolyn Cassady herself.) Libraries find these books to be precious repositories of literary history—"primary research," as scholars call such material. Budding literary critics find them even more exciting, because the information is entirely "unscreened" by inhibited New York-style editors. It is all served up respectfully, objectively and understandingly by the Knights, who have cultivated long-standing friendships with the people involved.

Last year upon meeting Allen Ginsberg at the COSMEP (Committee of Small Magazine Editors & Publishers) Conference held with the Knights' cooperation on their home campus of California State College in Pennsylvania, I asked the poet why they had access to so much sensitive material concerning him and Kerouac and Herbert Huncke and their likes. "Trustworthy people," Ginsberg said simply. "Absolutely trustworthy."

John Clellon Holmes (author of the fictionalized book, *Go*, concerning the adventures of the Ginsberg-Kerouac group in New York City during the late 1940s) feels the same way. He has provided the Knights with a generous sampling of his decades of correspondence with his lifelong friends, Kerouac and Ginsberg, as well as material reflecting on his own participation in the small group's birth in and around Columbia University during the years following World War II. All of this fascinating documentation appears in the journals that the Knights are publishing, mostly at their own expense out of sheer fervor for presenting firsthand recollections that could easily have been lost to the future. For this all of us interested in American letters owe them a debt of gratitude.

Strangely enough, neither Arthur's nor Kit's own poetry is what we have come to think of as Beat. There is no Zen-like appreciation of the landscape. These are obviously highly urban people. Their sexual interests are straight—they are completely wrapped up in their physical love for one another. They do not carouse, use dope, engage in anything that can be described as pornography, and they are committed to our institutionalized educational structure (Arthur is a very devoted teacher). They blame society for very little that is wrong, and nowhere do you find Society (with a capital) depicted as monstrously devilish, as in Kerouac, Ginsberg, Huncke. In their poetry, the Knights conservatively reiterate the classic maxim that individual character creates individual fate, and that most people's problems are simply what they deserve! A hard morality to follow, as the Classic Greeks discovered, and as the Chinese readers of Confucious protested. Of course this is what makes the Knights and their poetry so different in content (if not in conversational format) from their peers, who tend toward the kind of self-indulgent morality that blames others for insoluable personal problems. Sometimes this pragmatic philosophy makes harsh critics of humanity, but not in the case of Arthur and Kit Knight.

They are delightful companions, as my wife and I can testify to, having had them as guests in our home, and they are hosts of an almost Renaissance benevolence, which we have enjoyed as their guests occasionally—they do things for everyone they meet; they are almost universally liked and respected. They are gentleman and lady, a very unique commodity in our commercial culture, but without any of the bigoted squareness usually associated with these terms.

They can be as hip as Ginsberg, as frank as Miller, as tough as Williams, as precise as Emily Dickinson. They can discuss literature, politics, or the bag of garbage under their sink, or their love-life—all in poetic language that could still pass for conversation with a neighbor over their back fence. They are among the best of modern America's new voices.

—Westport CT, 1981

Honeymoons   Arthur Knight

"Honeymoons are for novices,"
you tell me
before falling asleep
on the way home
from Cumberland,
and I remember
the first time
I got married.
Veronica and I came home
to our new apartment
on Ashbury Street.
My parents had just finished
moving in our furniture,
so Veronica and I smiled
and told them
how glad we were
they were there.
The second time,
with Carole,
we went to Fort Bragg
but it was so foggy
we couldn't see the ocean.
Fumbling with her diaphragm,
she asked me to help her
get it in,
but I was never very mechanical.
The third time
Glee and I pulled a U-Haul
from Michigan to Pennsylvania,
where she spent the night
in the kitchen,
killing roaches
with a can of Raid.
You told me how
you honeymooned
with your first husband
in a trailor he'd rented.
You knew something was wrong,
watching the mosquitoes
swarm around the lights
that were supposed to
keep them away,
flies in your hair.
We eat dinner

at a restaurant where
the air conditioner's broken,
and it must be
a hundred outside.
You wipe the sweat and sleep
from your eyes.
When we get home
it's not as if
we're new to one another,
so you tell me
you don't want to
"do it" tonight.
Everyone does it
on honeymoons.
When I agree, I think
Corso would be proud of me.
But I still want you.
Even after
you've fallen asleep
I lie beside you
trying to
snub my erection.
I finger myself
thru the night.

Is the Garbage on Fire Yet?   Kit Knight

"I wish you hadn't done that,"
I said to Arthur as he dumped
the full ashtray into the garbage.
It was almost midnight
and Jim had just left
to start
his three-mile hike.
Arthur peered into the bag.
"*Ugh*.
Let the alley burn,"
he said, pulling the bag
out the back door. "The bones.
There're chicken bones in there
and dogs will tear it open—
I don't want garbage
all over the alley," I said.
"What'll we do?" Arthur asked,
standing in the alley
with a bag of chicken bones,
dirty diapers, and maybe
hot cigarette butts. "I want
to go to bed." "I have an idea,
but you'll probably think
it's silly," I said. "Go ahead,
tell me," Arthur said.
"Let's take it upstairs
to our room; then we won't
have to worry about it
being all alone." We dropped
it near the foot of the bed
by some crates we hadn't
unpacked yet. "When you're moving
you worry about the strangest things,"
Arthur said as he took off
his socks. "Where's the hamper?"
"I don't know—in the kitchen;
everything's in the kitchen,"
I answered. Thirty minutes later,
Arthur whispered,
"Is the garbage on fire yet?"

Philosophy — Arthur Knight

Your body's amber
as we lie
on the red rug
before the stove.
I've always liked night,
firelight,
and the smell of sex
and woodsmoke.
I carried logs
from the basement
before I tried to
fathom
what no man can,
my index finger
inside of you.
The tips of your nipples
glow like embers.
As I come I realize
I have lived all my life
for moments such as this.

Fat

Kit Knight

A thin friend says,
"A heavy person pays
a heavy price
in our culture."
I laughingly agree
with his wit, while
10 lbs hides quiveringly
under my smock. Handfuls
of vanilla wafers settle
among my ribs. I worry
while making love
that my thighs are too much
of an obstacle. I buy
grapefruit diet capsules
at the store and make
an enemy when the lady says,
"You don't have to worry."
I tell her, "Bullshit, too."

The Buy

Arthur Knight

I make the buy
for a dying friend.
Sitting at the hotel bar
where Yablonski's killers
holed up
before they hit him,
I look at the Monongahela
thru blue glass.
Talking to Lee
I watch the coal barges
move down river.
A 300-pound biker
in bib-overalls
and a hooker in her 40's
with dull blonde hair
(a quick one is still
five bucks in Appalachia)
sit at the bar,
The barmaid smiles;
she cleaned my kitchen once.
It is the closest
I've ever come
to anyone here.
I want to ask Lee
if there's more
to the lives of these people
than the dope and drink
they consume
to get them
thru the long afternoons,
or the quick encounters
in dusty rooms
where the mattresses
have a musty smell,
and the people come away
reeking of musk and cobwebs,
but I know it's hopeless.
I live in another land.
I give Lee the $10.00
and take the brown paper bag
and head for home,
five minutes
and 50,000 miles away.

Breast-feeding　　　　　　　　　　　　　　　Kit Knight

When I was nine
I discovered
women can feed their babies
thru their breasts.
I was delighted.
I tried it with my cat;
Boots wouldn't co-
operate. I have
a one-month-old baby
and am breast-weary
at 24. I nursed her
for the first two weeks
then quit, and no one told me
my breasts would swell
and hurt. No one told me
I'd still be leaking milk
for several months. There aren't
shots to dry up the milk
once it gets started.
Binding my breasts,
as my ob suggested,
was mummifying.
A woman who is breast-feeding
cannot take the pill. Why didn't
someone tell me that
before I started to nurse?
Arthur and I went
to childbirth education classes—
what was the point?
Tiffany is asleep in her crib
after taking six ounces of formula.
I'm tired of listening
to breast-feeding women
tell me how inconspicuous
nursing in public can be
and that only two per cent
of all jailbirds were breast-fed.
Boots was a smart cat.

A Great Place To Be

Arthur Knight

Each time I go back
to San Francisco
I get a toothache,
and there're armed guards
in the halls
of all the high schools,
but it isn't snowing.
Each time I go back
the people are more afraid
to walk the streets at night,
altho you hear them talking
in the Safeway
about how
they wouldn't live
anywhere else,
and it isn't snowing.
The people we know tell us
it's a great place to be
because of all
the cultural advantages,
altho they're all so poor
from high mortgage payments
that the most cultural thing
they can afford
is a Basque dinner
in North Beach
one Sunday each month,
but it isn't snowing.
Each time I go back
the pimps stand
on the corners,
and the junkies
don't have to wear overcoats
waiting for connections
and North Beach really is
pretty at night,
altho it's not
what it used to be.
The cops don't have
a sense of humor anymore,
arresting A. D.
for taking a joyride
he was too drunk to remember
in a stolen taxi.
And one of the lights

that forms a nipple
on Carol Doda's titties
isn't twinkling,
but someone will probably
fix it soon,
everyone has reason
to believe.
It never snows.

The Magic Day
Kit Knight

I'm hungry and I want
an ice cream bar.
At Christmas I weighed
108 lbs. and now
for Valentine's Day I weigh
116 lbs. I'd like
a root beet float, too.
Made with ice milk
and sugarless soda, please.
I'd also like a cigarette
to replace
the tar in my lungs
with the guilt in my head.
My mother-in-law tells me,
casually, of course,
the walls in the living room
have to be washed more often
when a smoker has been around.
There's a box of tiny gumdrops
sitting on the counter
(and I hear
all those grape and cherry voices).
My baby daughter brings me
her story books
and I shake my head and frown.
She puckers up
and I feel guilty.
Was today the magic day
for learning the difference
between a gobble and a quack?
Arthur senses my unhappiness;
he's unnecessarily short
with Tiffany and when I hear
her cries—even tho I know
she isn't hurt—I feel guilty.
I couldn't smoke if I wanted
to anyway. Matt is coming
to visit and bringing his son—
and the kid is asthmatic,
can't stand a smoker in the room.
Not to mention the walls,
of course. And I've been stuck
in the house for the last two weeks
blowing my nose. The Eskimos
call it pibloktu. Someone else
called it "cabin fever."
I call it stuck.

Scars Arthur Knight

An eight inch scar
curves across
your right leg,
and somebody else's bone
is where your kneecap
used to be,
grafted there.
At the lower corner
of your left lip
there is a smaller scar,
barely noticeable,
the only
facial evidence remaining.
The plastic surgeon's art
hides the rest.
After nine years
you look up
the name of the driver
who hit you—
Beam—
but his name isn't listed
in the phone book anymore.
It is as if
he never existed,
but at night, especially,
your leg still throbs.

Russian Christmas   Kit Knight

I'm half-Ukranian; both
my mother's parents
came from "Little Russia."
Of course, neither of them
lived to see their granddaughter;
in fact, my mother's father
didn't live long enough
to see her. But my grandmother
did live long enough to bequeath
the hideous Clahanees to me
(via her influence over
my mother), I was told
the Clahanees were big-
breasted women who lived
in the woods and only
came out to give
the evil eye; they lived
year around, but were particularly
prevalent in December
and able to fuck-up
the entire coming year
if they looked at you.
My aunt saw one once
in the supermarket
near the jumbo (baloney).
"The Clahanees are coming;
quick," she said,
"get the garlic & salt."
Prayer works too—
"Oh, sweet Jesus."
American me knows
it's all bullshit—
but the fact remains,
I did absorb it.

John Wayne is Dying　　　　　　　　　　　　　　　Arthur Knight

John Wayne is dying
the announcer says.
Driving home in the rain
I'm surprised Kit can sleep,
Nine years ago today
she was hit by a car
as she crossed the street.
She was in a coma
for nine weeks.
And her favorite aunt
died on the same date
five years later.
On the freeway
ahead of us
there's a wreck,
and the announcer says
the subway train
caught on fire
in the tube between
Oakland and San Francisco,
and no one knows why.
No one knows why.
I'm 41 years old,
and I can't remember
a time when
John Wayne wasn't a star,
but I can remember when
they built the subway,
and I don't like any of it:
the rain
or Kit's accident
or even her aunt,
whom I never knew,
dying,
or the fire in the subway
or Kit's pain
as she tries to
kick cigarettes.
John Wayne is dying.

A Valentine's Day Poem for Mark   Kit Knight

All he ever did
was watch Tarzan movies,
build plastic ship models,
shop at K-Mart,
talk about what a great
arm wrestler his dad was
(from pulling the whistle
in a train engine),
occasionally fumble
in bed, and go out to eat
at Dean's Diner.
And people ask me,
why did I get a divorce?

Sweet Potato Arthur Knight
    for Dad

You were the last
of three children,
ten years younger
than your brother,
and you grew-up knowing
you weren't wanted,
always in the backseat
of your parents' car
as if you were
someone undiscovered.
"Children are seen, not heard."
Sick from gas fumes,
you'd vomit by the roadside.

You left home immediately
when you got out of high school
You disappointed your parents,
going to Heald's Business College.
They'd always known
you'd go to Cal. Instead
you went to see
the Solons play at night
and spent tropical evenings
in the valley playing pool.

Mom says you met a girl
who died an alcoholic
and you never drank much
after that.
She never told me why
you gave up your dream
to write. You worked for
Pacific Fruit and Produce,
taking shorthand
when you weren't
unloading boxcars.
It was during the Depression.
Maybe that explains it.
Maybe not.

When I was born
you were almost ready
to have a nervous breakdown.
Sixteen hour days
seven days a week

are too much for any man.
In the evenings you played
the sweet potato,
and I remember you sitting
on the front steps
cutting warts from your thumb
with a jackknife.
There were games of kick-the-can.

When I entered high school
you and mom ended-up
taking care of your parents
because your brother wouldn't
and your sister was dead.

Your father had a stroke
and your mother was confined
to a wheelchair,
and you and mom
only went away once overnight
in the next few years.
Grandpa tried to read the paper
upside-down, and choked
until his false teeth rattled,
living on bananas and baby food.

When I went to college
I smoked and drank too much
—or at least you thought so—
and there were the women
you never seemed to like.
I sent you letters
telling you not to worry,
but you always did.
When I told you
I wanted to be a writer
it was as if some part of your past
you'd lobotomized came back.
It was an impossible dream.

"Get a job."

I sold the Ford convertible
you'd given me
and went to Europe,
one marriage already behind me.
The first in our family
to be divorced,

making history in my twenties.
I did it again
within three years.
No one was proud of me.
And you said I was
"an educated bum"
before I moved east.
I left a note on your door
saying goodbye.
Mom told me later
you cried when you read it.

It was ten years before
we'd see each other again.
I came back with the woman
who'd be my fourth wife,
sleeping down the hall with her
from the room you and mom shared.
She said you told her,
"Arthur's an adult now."

You'd sold the business you'd had
more than twenty years,
becoming a botanist
because it was something
you wanted to do.
I wondered how you'd managed
to sell venetian blinds and rugs
so many years.
Water on the knee
from laying carpet.
How does anyone survive
meaningless work?

Last weekend you phoned
to tell us
you've finally retired,
that you and mom
are selling the house
and moving here.
It won't be long
before you're teaching our daughter
how to grow things
and describing her daddy's boyhood—
we wore dogtags in elementary school
in case there was a Jap invasion—
and your own.
Born before the radio existed,

you broke your arm
cranking a Model T.

Things change and remain the same.
I can see you at the end of summer
sitting on the swing
as the street lights filter thru
the large maples in our yard
playing my daughter
the same songs you played me
forty years ago
on the sweet potato.

That Clean Sun Smell   Kit Knight

"So early in the morning"—
the last line
of the nursery rhyme
sings thru my mind
as I watch
the woman next door
hanging her son's baby briefs
on the clothesline.
The woman on the other side
has towels flapping
in the summer wind.
I was only ten
the last time I had to
pin clothes on a line.
Mommy was the first
in our housing project
to have a dryer. I remember
my aunt saying, "Nothing beats
that clean sun smell."
A few years later
my aunt got her dryer.
And a few years after that
my aunt was dead. I guess
nothing does beat
that clean sun smell.

Woman of the Year   Arthur Knight

Kit's mother may be
Woman of the Year,
and Helen is excited
about the possibility,
altho she says
the members of her club
insisted
she accept the nomination.
Helen will almost certainly
have to buy a new dress
for the occasion,
and she has already told us
she's getting new drapes
for her front room,
altho we can see
nothing wrong with
those she now has.
Helen has purchased
a blue umbrella
for our daughter
because she is
starting her second year
in nursery school,
and Helen has given
her other two grandchildren
new things for the new year,
altho she and Basil
have not been to see us
in more than three months
because they can't afford
the gas for an hour's drive.
We have been asked
to loan them
a thousand dollars,
altho Helen helped
Kit's first husband
try to kidnap her
when the marriage was ending,
and when Kit
moved in with me,
her mother told her
it was really too bad
Kit's attempted suicide
had failed. Her mother said

I was a sonofabitch,
and she would never
call me son.
Now Kit has the key
to her parents' home again,
and the last birthday card
I received from Helen
was signed Mom.
A thousand dollars
isn't really much
in this economy,
and Basil has been laid off,
and we will almost certainly
be seeing
Helen's photo in the paper
because she has given to
the volunteer fire department
and to the ambulance service
and Helen has given generously
of her time,
which she has so much of,
to any organization,
and she is a member
in good standing
at the Catholic church
she never attends,
and we could borrow the money
if we don't have it.
Helen understands.
We'll all be *so* proud of her
when she is
Woman of the Year.

Symbols Kit Knight

Symbols convey information.
Letters on a page,
traffic signs.
I don't like it
when symbols are used
to say something
that doesn't really exist.
Pudgy Pat is president
of the nursery school
my daughter attends.
I listen to Pat complain
about high prices
and the cost of gas.
Her sons ride bicycles.
And her husband left her
for someone slimmer
who hasn't lived long enough
to be a complainer.
The town of Coal Center
looks like it sounds
—shabby. Yesterday was
the muggiest day of June,
and Pat told me
how uncomfortable it was
to walk home
and how much she enjoyed
drinking her Perrier water.

Memorial Day — Arthur Knight

Our welfare neighbors
watch their two sons
play in the wading pool,
two tiny American flags
alongside it,
while I pick up
the dead rose branches
my father-in-law pruned
from the bushes
behind our home.
I'm unaccountably depressed,
as my wife was last night
when her mother left.
At best
we nod at our neighbors,
passing in the alley,
our belief one should work
evident on our faces.
We try to conceal our scorn.
At best we do not argue
with my mother-in-law,
telling ourselves
her paralysing
lack of interest in others
is just her way.
When the Legionnaires
fired their rifles
near the monument
commemorating the fallen
this morning
I wondered why
it is so much easier
to honor our dead
than it is to respect
those who still live.

Memorial Day Rose Kit Knight

A friend of ours
signed a letter with,
"Say a prayer
for the hostages—
even if it's a first."
Last year
Ohio suffered
severe blizzards.
The governor asked
all the residents
to pray
for divine intervention.
Both requests seemed,
to me,
equally silly.
What's more important
is the single red rose
that magically appeared
on the bush overhanging
the swing on our front porch.

The Picnic   Arthur Knight
   for John Paul Minarik

John touches his wife's hair
as they sit
next to one another
at the picnic table
in front of the prison.
An armed guard,
stationed across the yard
watches each move John makes.
This is no movie,
but if I were to film it
it is a picture
I would make
in black and white.
Kit gives John's daughters
jellybeans
we were not allowed to take
into the prison earlier.
We are continually amazed
at the things
John cannot have,
at the things
John cannot do.
He has told us
what it was like
buying a postage stamp
after more than ten years.
Someone must have said
let him enjoy his freedom
thirty-seven days,
then bring him back.
Getting soft buys no votes
in an election year.
It's beginning to rain
when we leave.
John shakes my hand
and he and Kit hug,
the walls of the prison
one hundred feet behind them.
It is like no picnic
I have ever imagined,
and I drive home
faster than I should
in the hard rain.

Specific Detail   Kit Knight

Passing the exit to Pittsburgh
we continued driving on I 79,
heading toward Western Penitentiary.
Arthur waited
for my always effusive comments
on that stretch of highway.
I'm always in awe
of the engineering feat
it must have taken
to drive that road
straight thru the rocks,
sort of like Moses.
After he finished the Red Sea,
did he travel I 79?

I've got a bag of jellybeans
to give the prisoners
during the poetry discussion.
Guards tell me
I can't take it in—
I suppose I could have
sat and injected all 100
with a drug. Walking thru
the main yard I'm very aware
that all five feet of my body
is closely inspected
by the prisoners and the guards.
But no one whistles
and if there are any leers,
they come from the guards.
Does one feel safer
with a gun? Our guide suggested
I not wear a dress
but I'm not any more comfortable
in pink slacks and white heels.
The hot pink clashes
with the dark khaki uniforms
the prisoners must wear.
Perhaps I should have worn
something charming in stripes.

Paul also lets us have
a quick look at the cell blocks.
If one adds six inches
to the width and length
of my queensize bed—

that is the size of each cell.

The convicts read us
poetry they have written,
and we try to explain
the need for a character
to do something. I say,
"Specific detail,"
over and over.
By the end
of our three-day visit
I feel like a harper.

The brown khaki shirt
our host is wearing
is harsh to my cheek
when I hug him goodby
at the locked gate
topped with barbwire
that separates
the free from the non-free.
John Minarik says, "Careful,
they'll shoot."

Destruction   Arthur Knight

One did it by going crazy,
believing Swedenborg
talked to angels in trees;
another did it by
not going to the doctor,
letting herself explode
internally, day by day,
taking massive amounts
of cortisone;
another did it by drinking
night after night:
whiskey and beer,
or sometimes she did it
with gin;
it didn't matter.
All the processes
were the same.

I watch you
lie on the couch
all afternoon;
you smoke cigarettes,
after being off them
for months,
staring out the window.
You complain
about the same thing
the others did:
growing old,
the same futility.
You say you haven't
done anything,
not knowing exactly
what it is
you want to do,
and I watch you
helpless;
this is not deja vu.
I've been there before,
but it gets no easier.

The Result   Kit Knight

Sandy was the result of an affair
between her Chinese mother's
first and second marriages.
Sandy's father was one of those
good-looking white men who
"don't want no Chink kid."
Carole's second husband
was also a white man and
Arthur adopted Sandy, age four
and already emotionally overweight.
While Carole haunted all the
Catholic churches (sure she was
possessed), the illegitimate half-
breed child looked for Santa Claus
under a palm tree on a Los Angeles Blvd.

Constellations Arthur Knight

I rock, naked,
on the upstairs porch,
watching
the lights go out
one by one.
It is just after eleven
when Kit joins me;
wearing her baby-doll top,
she sits on my lap.
There is a half-moon,
diffused by the mist,
and I feel myself grow
as we watch
the constellations,
rocking gently.
Our bodies fold
into one another.
We begin
our fourth year.
Rocking. Rocking.

His Grandson Is Uneasy   Kit Knights

We got a letter from Karl
last week and he told us
his cancer had spread
from his lung
to his elbow, hip and spleen.
He talked about Carolyn,
his latest love.
Karl's love life is difficult
to chronicle because he has
three ex-wives and
five kids. He tells us
his grandson is uneasy
about Karl's approaching death.
The boy is only six.
How does one explain?
What can one say?
When Karl lived in this town
(two blocks away), I always
had a reason not to go
see him. I was uneasy
with his approaching death.
I didn't know what to say.
I kept him supplied with
cookies and brownies, tho,
which I sent over
with my husband.
People seem to believe
writers shouldn't ever
have problems knowing
what to say. But I honestly
didn't know what to say.
In his letter, Karl seemed
reconciled to his approaching
death. But he also spoke
of going to the Yucatan Peninsula
to visit the Mayan ruins
because, as he put it,
"I'd rather see them
than be one."
Karl ended his letter with,
"I rather hope to be around
to welcome you at Xmas time."
Yes, Karl—Arthur and I
would like to see you, too.
As a human being
is it my duty
to deliberately put myself
in a position of uneasiness?

The Cache   Arthur Knight

When the pain
becomes too great
Karl tells us
he'll kill himself,
and he spills
a bottle of percodan
across his bed,
determined not to be
a burden to his kids,
determined not to
spend his last days
in a cancer ward,
dying among strangers,
not knowing
whether he smells
his own decaying flesh
or someone else's,
not knowing
whether he hears
his own screams
in the night
or someone else's.
He tells us this
matter-of-factly,
as if he is talking
about going to
the beach tomorrow.
When we leave,
we try not to
look at the pills
spread across his bed
in the dread light.
We tell him
we'll see him again,
and he says
he hopes so;
he honestly hopes so.

Summer Roses   Kit Knight

We haven't done it,
yet. It's been over a year
since we first sat
on the upstairs porch.
Neatly shaded
from curious eyes
by tall maples.
I've never made love outdoors,
except once,
in a motel pool
near Oklahoma City.
Cowboys and Indians wandering
on the streets below.
When Arthur came
I watched the cum float away.
Anti-abortionists would call that
"the drowning of pre-born life."
I just thought it was pretty.
It wasn't time yet
for our baby to be conceived.

Tonite we're going to spread
sheets and blankets on the floor
of the old wooden porch.
Going to push the lawn chairs
far to the side. Cool breezes
will nuzzle our skins,
somehow, I know,
better than
our air-conditioned bedroom.
Summer roses trail
one side of the porch.
The air will be sweet
with honeysuckle and sex.
Sitting here typing this poem,
listening to our daughter
laugh at Big Bird,
I watch the sun set.

The Breakdown   Arthur Knight

Marilyn hallucinates
at the end
of a five-day drunk;
blood gushes
from beneath her nails.
Bob's little girls
are scared.
Marilyn doesn't know
her real parents,
altho she thinks
she might have met them
two years ago
on a rainy afternoon
in Portland, Oregon.
Marilyn has told her friends
she believes Bob is
a latent homosexual
because he is
passive in bed.
Marilyn hallucinates
Elizabeth Taylor Warner,
both of them overweight;
and Bob was interested
in politics
when they met:
Vice Major of Petaluma.
Marilyn hallucinates.
When the cops come
they handcuff her,
but she goes out kicking.
At Oakcrest
150 out of 200 psychiatrists
are Jews,
and Marilyn believes
they persectue her
to get even for
what happened to them
in Doozledorf.
They drug her.
They put her in
a strait jacket.
Marilyn does not hallucinate.

A Nice Thing To Do
Kit Knight

Our daughter started to go
to nursery school this September.
Her first institution
of higher learning.
Last night her father
and I attended
an executive board meeting
of the nursery school.
Arthur was the only man
present and the meeting
had to be dismissed
by 9 so the bar patrons
could watch the football game.
Donna, the executive president,
lives in Daisytown;
we don't know which house,
but Daisytown has quite a few
functional outhouses.
(I wonder
do they use Sears' catalogs?)
After about an hour
someone said her little boy
had mentioned that they
were no longer saying
grace before their snacks.
And she asked why.
The teacher, Alice, said
some parents had objected;
and all 18 ladies nodded
and agreed
saying grace was a nice thing to do.
Arthur and I were the villains.
I was even wearing
black slacks. We said,
"Saying grace belongs
in the home or at church,
not in a nondenominational school."
A lady with red hair
and a pink blouse
that she'd outgrown two sizes ago
said, "We always
have said grace in nursery school
and isn't it in the by-laws?"
Alice answered, "Yes, we always have
but that doesn't mean we should;

and, no, it isn't written in the by-laws."
One of the teacher's aids said,
"To keep peace,
would it be agreeable
if I took Tiffany out
for a small walk in the hall
while the other children
were saying grace?"
"No," Arthur answered.
"She'd feel like a freak.
I've seen Jehovah's Witnesses' kids
who were only required
to stand
while the rest of the kids
recited the Pledge of Allegiance
and they felt foolish."
The outhouse president suggested
that we pull our daughter out
of nursery school if we objected
that much. Alice finally said,
"The purpose of nursery school
is not to teach grace.
So that's it, we won't
say grace anymore."
The ladies were silent.
"The lord hath spoken,"
I whispered to Arthur.

Promise Me Arthur Knight

Vanessa was afraid
Boyd would find out
she'd come over,
but she needed
diapers for the baby.
As soon as she came in
she apologized
for the way she looked,
telling Kit
she'd had to
sneak out
thru the basement.
Boyd had told her
never to borrow anything,
but he was out of work
and she didn't know
what to do.
They talked less
each day now,
and Boyd would take off
for long walks,
not telling her
where he went,
and he didn't like her
phoning people,
asking
if they'd seen him.
When she'd called here
one night
she made me promise
not to say anything,
and now Kit had to
reassure her.
"Promise me you won't
tell I was here,"
Vanessa said,
"promise me."

Horror Stories   Kit Knight

"Even the music is from
crudsville," I said as I watched
Night of the Living Dead
from the door. Arthur sat
on the couch and said,
"It'll blow your socks off—
come watch it."
It was the night before
Halloween and the movie
was supposed to set the tone.
I had stayed upstairs
and washed my panty hose
so I wouldn't see the movie.
I had stood beside
my daughter's crib and watched
her sleep—peacefully unaware
of the zombies crawling around
downtown Pittsburgh,
only an hour away—
so I wouldn't see the movie.
Never liked horror shows.
I still keep my closet door
shut at night. I used
to wear a little gold cross
around my neck;
it was nicer than garlic.

Kevin Arthur Knight

Before he went
into the psychiatric ward
he had no idea
what was happening
or why.
It was as if
he were reading
about someone else.
All summer long
he kept winning
the patient of the week award,
sure he'd never be
honored again.
He'd gnash his teeth at night,
smoke all day long,
and dream about the nurses.
He remembered
the two of us
sitting in his driveway
the day before
he was institutionalized.
He felt he was
going down with the sun.
I tried to talk to him,
but didn't know
what to say.
What can you tell someone?
"We all have our hells."
He tells me
how it is teaching,
how much better
his life has become,
altho he still
gnashes his teeth at night,
sometimes,
and awakens
spitting blood.

Two Women   Kit Knight

Leaning on the cash register
surrounded by
Revlon and City cosmetics—
two for $5, a sign frantically
tells me—we listen
to the women talk
as they ring up sales.
Trina, who is lovely enough
to be snobbish, asks
if I believe in love
at first sight. Firmly,
I answer, no; however
I do believe
in attraction at first sight.
Charlotte totals the amount
for the lipsticks and complains
she can't fall in love.
Upon closer questioning
I realize
it's Charlotte's parents
who tell her
she can't fall in love.
They fear
she will get married again
then get divorced again.
Charlotte gets irritated
by their not-so-subtle questions.
Then defends them by saying,
"But I need them for babysitting."
I volunteer, "(a) Tell them
as little as possible, and (b)
tell them less." Privately,
I wonder why this teenager
can't babysit himself.
Trina says, "I have given
my entire life over to serving
my husband and two daughters,
one 18 and the other 21.
Now I realize
they're about gone
and no one is going to serve me."
The store will close soon
and Trina tells us,
"I like Heineken beer."

40

We say good-by
and hand-in-hand
Arthur and I leave;
he says, "The first guy
who is right for Trina
and asks her to go
have a Heineken—
she'll be gone." I agree,
Trina has the restless look,
the look of one who's been had,
doesn't like it,
and plans to do something.

Just like somebody I knew
a long time ago.
I squeeze Arthur's hand.

The Thief
Arthur Knight

Kit sits in the bathtub
crying
because there is snow
outside.
One knee was broken twice
and the other
broken once,
and ten years later
Kit is still unsure
of her footing. She says,
"The snow is a thief;
it robs me
of the little mobility
I usually have."
For almost a month
Kit has been
buying the groceries
and picking up our mail
at the post office
because I have had
pneumonia. She performs
my tasks with difficulty
even in good weather.
Kit is not used to
walking so much.
At night her legs hurt
and she has to
elevate them on a pillow
as she sleeps.
When there is snow
walking becomes impossible.
Sitting in the tub
Kit watches the snow
realizing it will end,
but not soon enough
to help her make it
thru this day.
Kit knows when
she has been robbed.
She cries.

Breakfast   Kit Knight

I awaken to the sound
of a body thumping down
the curved staircase.
Our 50-lb. puppy
has been penned-up
on the balcony porch
for the night
and she has to pee.
Arthur hurries to open
the front door for her,
but the damn dog
is so excited . . .
I hear Arthur shouting,
"No, no. Bad dog,"
and I know
the throw rug will be
ignominiously heaped
in the washing machine.
I drift back to sleep—
almost—
then I hear
the Apple Jacks cereal song
seeping under the door
of the baby's room.
I open one eye to squint
at the clock and think,
shit,
I never have my glasses
when I need them.

Petting Arthur Knight

I run my hands
along your back,
massaging your shoulder;
I trace a line
along your spine,
watching your flesh
ripple.
It has been
more than three years
since the first night.
You like the petting
more than the sex,
you told me.
Most things are
different now.
There is the baby,
and the sex is better,
but your breath
still catches,
coming more quickly
when I touch you.

Bananas Are for Dead People   Kit Knight

"I only want a half,"
my daughter yelled
from the living room.
The other half looked sad
lying there by itself,
sort of divided. So
I sliced it into
my husband's Cheerios
and poured the orange juice.
Arthur stamped into the kitchen
leaving puddles of snow
around the door.
"I don't want bananas
on my cereal." His words
snapped and I jumped.
"But everybody puts bananas
on their cereal—besides
Tiffany only wanted half,"
I answered. I listened as
his voice took on
a different tone,
one I'd seldom heard.
"Bananas were about all
my grandfather could eat,
toward the end.
Bananas are for dead people."

Bailing   Arthur Knight

You asked
if I wanted to
fool around
last night,
and I told you
it was too hot
and I was tired.
During the night
it rained, and
when we got up
this morning
we began
to bail out
the water
around our furnace
in the basement.
"This is what
home ownership
is all about"
you tell me.
We use the buckets
we bought
to pick berries,
dumping the water
into our daughter's
wading pool.
I watch the outline
of your nipples
against white cotton,
watch your breasts
shift
as you bail.
It is too late
to change my mind.

The Queen Lives on Unemployment   Kit Knight

Rebecca listens to her parents
wondering
if the check will arrive.
Her dad's been laid-off
for over a month,
Jack's beer-bloated belly
is getting bigger.
The little girl just started
kindergarten; she likes
to play school
on their grimy front steps.
And my three-year-old
makes a perfect pupil.
I listen to Rebecca explain,
"Now class, today
we are going to learn
about apples. This
is an A. No, no,
not upside down—
you make it this way."
Today,
Rebecca is a teacher.
Yesterday,
I listened to Rebecca
telling my daughter
about kings and queens.
And she fashioned for herself
a crown made of
used tinfoil.

Simple Things   Arthur Knight

The simple things:
listening to Kit sing
as she bathes the baby:
"Toot, toot, Tootsie,
don't cry,"
and the cicadas' sound,
the rockers
creaking in the wind
side by side
on the porch upstairs.
I was born and raised
in San Francisco,
and moved fast there:
sixty miles an hour
out Geary one night,
crazy drunk. 1960.
Looking.
I stand on the porch
drinking a beer. Here,
the grass green as it is
in a Rockwell painting,
no one is on the street.
I listen to Kit sing.
Simple things.

Up With the Bourgeois   Kit Knight

Sitting on cushions
nervously watching
to be sure someone didn't
knock over
a lit candle
while reaching for
a cold picece of pizza
the cat had been sniffing,
watching the joint make the rounds
of 20 some people
sitting on the floor
of a drafty room
that is only comfortable for five.
Karl told us
the Cloudhouse looked like
all the neighborhood dogs
had gone there to die.
This party was supposed to be
a farewell to the Cloudhouse.
The "in" house of the 50's
was closing its doors.
I signaled to Gerry
that I was ready to leave.
Ready to return
to my house with two bathrooms
and electric lights.

On the Road   Arthur Knight

We don't make love
in Iowa City,
altho I'm always hot
on the road.
We drive across the midwest
with our windows down,
and Kit ties my handkerchief
around my wrist
so it won't burn.
We sip Slush Puppies
in the 100 degree heat,
our lips purple
hours later
in the neon light
of our bathroom
at the Motel 6.
I have a hard-on
and the beginning
of a headache.
When we go for a swim,
I remember the summer
we made love in a pool,
but this one's crowded
and we end-up talking
to a woman who says
she's a minister
who writes poetry.
After dinner
and a few beers,
my headache's gone
but my hard-on isn't,
and I don't know why.
After the heat
and the Slush Puppies,
and the fat girls
who pump gas
wearing T-shirts with
their nipples protruding
thru Kenny Rogers' eyeballs,
after the Stucky's that appear
like mirages in the middle
of the cornfields,
I don't know why.
I'm always hot on the road.

Ink Stains Kit Knight

"Only a true writer
would get ink stains
in his underwear,"
I said as I watched
Arthur wash off
the little face
I had drawn
on the tip
of his penis
with a purple Flair.

Denial   Arthur Knight

In the old days I could
drink a dozen beers,
eat a bag of potato chips,
and smile
when I weighed-in,
but middle-age comes at you
like a punch-drunk fighter,
and the pounds pile-up
around the waist.
Now it's 3 light beers
and sit-ups,
and I flinch a little
when I pass the potato chips.
Getting old takes
getting used to.
At dinner I eat more salads
and switch to oil and vinegar,
and I've consumed so many
steamed vegetables
I think I'll turn green.
When we make love
I wonder if I ought to
take the bottom,
and when I go by bars
I always walk
a little faster,
but the pounds pile-up
like the days of our lives,
and nothing—nothing—
is easy anymore.

Too Old to Be Sexy   Kit Knight

Getting dressed
to go to stand
behind my table of books
at the New York Book Fair and
sell / smile / shake hands and
SMILE—I looked at
my white high heels and
my pink form-fitting shirt.
Then I thought about
having to walk to the subway
and jumping on and off
the trains. I decided
on sensible shoes. Then I
looked at the rain and decided
it was really too cool
to wear a sleeveless shirt;
I pulled a plain pullover
out of my suitcase.
I can remember a time—
less than ten years ago—
when it simply didn't matter.